THE ART OF DRAWING

MANGA

BEN KREFTA

THE ART OF DRAWING

MANGA

BEN KREFTA

BARNES
&NOBLE
BOOKS
NEW YORK

This edition published by Barnes & Noble, Inc.
by arrangement with
Arcturus Publishing Limited
26/27 Bickels Yard, 151–153 Bermondsey Street,
London SE1 3HA

2003 Barnes & Noble Books

M 10 9 8 7 6 5 4 3 2 1

ISBN 0-7607-4693-1

Cover and book design by Steve Flight
Artwork Ben Krefta

Printed and bound in China

ACKNOWLEDGEMENTS

I would like to thank the following for their invaluable help in
creating this book:

Kim Loh from Malaysia

webmaster@neo-epiphani.com

website: http://www.neo-epiphani.com

Kim created the groovy red bikini girl (page 71).

&

Dan Fielding aka Cloud from the UK

cloudstrife@yahoo.com

website: http://www.cloudsgallery.com

Dan is the talented artist of the warrior maid (page 81),
the running girl (page 97) and the action pic of the girl
with two guns (page 142).

Last but not least a big thanks to my brother James Krefta for his
invaluable help in putting the text together.

ENTS

INTROD

Times are changing – exciting 'anime' and 'manga' artwork has finally been recognized here in the west for its exotic designs, flair and wonderfully distinct style. Nowadays we often see it in entertainment media such as magazines, comic books, television, advertising, graphic design and websites, and even at the movies. Yet not so long ago it was a genre of art restricted to audiences in Asia.

What are these art forms?

Basically, manga are comic books and the word 'anime' means animation. When these Japanese terms are used they generally refer to original Japanese creations and not those created elsewhere. However, so many people all over the world are being inspired by the manga style that such work now has its own descriptive title – 'Pseudo Manga'.

'Manga' literally translates as 'irresponsible pictures' and it is argued that the first examples were Chinese temple wall paintings of Shaolin monks practicing martial arts. More recently, Japanese comics proved popular throughout the 1960s with the serialization of numerous stories, including Osamu Tezuka's 'Mighty Atom', which later became a long-running anime between 1963–1966.

Ironically, the origins of early Japanese animation was heavily influenced by American cartoons of the 1950s – Betty Boop for example, with her big wide eyes. These were adapted by Japanese artists and are a notable inspiration for modern anime character design.

Why has it become so popular and how is it different from western comics?

Within Japanese culture it has been a widely accepted art style for many years and it's here that 'manga' was born. Manga artists and writers are celebrated as much as best-selling authors and artists are here in the west. Every week in Japan, huge volumes are printed and read by millions of people of all ages. Indeed, its popularity is largely attributed to the diversity of genres that appeal to every age and gender. Subjects can vary from romance to high school sports teams, outer space battles with huge mechanical warriors to occult horror, even traditional folk lore to name but a few.

UCTION

It is here that we notice the first difference to western comics; few manga are based on superheroes but tend to focus on average people thrust into abnormal circumstances. Perhaps we have come to identify more closely with the manga characters because they are so different from the superheroes in stories and art style we are accustomed to.

Technically there are several key differences between the art of western comics and manga. Manga tends to rely less on heavy shading and utilizes smooth line-art. While the characters often appear simplistic in the way they are drawn, the overall attention to detail is astounding, especially in the backgrounds where the picture is composed as a whole entity rather than aspects added as an afterthought. Then there is the humor in manga – even if the story is not a comedy, several artistic conventions are often used to emphasize the gestures and expressions of characters.

Examples include the big sweat drop on the brow indicating tension, the small mushroom-shaped cloud from the mouth depicting relief, and a bulging vein at the side of the head to convey frustration and anger.

Many western artists and publishers are now producing pseudo manga and releasing original titles. This isn't a case of 'jumping on the band wagon' – it is because we like what is offered by the medium, its freshness and excitement. Manga isn't a fad, manga is here to stay!

In this book you are treated to step-by-step instructions on how to create manga illustrations. The style is suitable for manga, anime or video game design, and is in keeping with the most popular Japanese techniques and aesthetics. The approach is intended for novice manga artists who have some basic knowledge of drawing. It is presented in a way that should be helpful if you are learning for the first time. As such, the sections are broken down to focus on particular

areas – the male/female head, face, hair and body. Then the budding artist can move on to character clothing and accessories, building up to designing your own characters.

The hope is that you will enjoy this book and have a lot of fun generating wonderful manga artwork. The key to creating accomplished artwork is to keep practicing. With this solid grounding you'll soon produce manga as good as that of your

favorite professionals. Keep this thought in mind – there was a time when even THEY couldn't draw for candy! Everyone has to start somewhere…

MATE
& TOO

I f you're new to drawing and just want to dig in you'll only need three basic items: a pencil, an eraser and paper. When you become more skilled and confident at drawing it's good to experiment with better quality materials and different tools to make the most of your work.

Using good quality materials will give better results and enhance your picture. The next stage should be to use several pencils of varying densities for shading purposes and heavier grade paper.

You may want to ink and color your pictures, in which case you'll use more tools for those tasks, all of which are detailed in this section.

Experienced artists have their own preferences for materials, depending on their style and favorite medium. This is something you'll develop over time, but in the meantime have some fun playing around with different materials. It's just as important to discover a material you don't like as it is to find a material you love.

On the following pages we'll go through the array of materials you can use as a manga artist and outline what we consider to be the advantages and disadvantages of using each medium. The pros and cons of each medium shouldn't be matched against one another to find the 'perfect tool', but merely taken as points to consider.

Pencils

The first tool you'll need to acquire is a pencil – ideally a range of pencils varying from a hard 3H to a soft 2B. In manga artwork you need to maintain smooth, clean lines so using anything darker than 2B will result in smudging which cannot be removed easily with an eraser. Not only that, but clean line-art makes the inking stage easier (where black outlines are put down on the illustration and shadows are added).

Whether you use a mechanical pencil or ordinary wooden one, pencils are the standard medium used to draw manga, from layouts and sketches to the final illustration, so it's crucial to practice using them.

Advantages

① Even if you're new to drawing manga, chances are you've used pencils before so it's a medium you'll already have experience with.

② If drawn lightly, pencil marks can be removed with a soft eraser or putty rubber so shapes can be redrawn until they look right.

Disadvantages

① Plan out your drawing on scrap paper before committing to the final sheet because if you make too many mistakes and rub them out, it can leave permanent marks.

② Pencil gives an inconsistent line depending on the pressure you apply. This can make it tricky to maintain the shape and tone of a line. This is especially evident with soft pencils.

Pens

Pens can be divided into two major types: quill pens and ballpoint pens. Quill pens draw lines that have depth. The ballpoint pen gives clean, consistent lines and is a lot simpler to use.

If you look at a manga drawing closely, you will notice that the line thickness is often inconsistent, with lines thinning near the end. Create this effect by controlling the pressure exerted on the pen. Quill pens, if used correctly, give nice delicate lines and a lot of depth to your illustration. Rotring rapidograph pens tend to be used for drafting purposes, but work really well for manga too so use them! You don't have to worry about dipping the pen in the ink and the line texture is always consistent.

Erasers

You'll probably use this more than you want to but remember, erasing mistakes is not a bad thing! Residue from erasers may spoil the tone effect if it remains on the paper so be sure to keep your desktop very clean. You may want to purchase a pen-type eraser to help in erasing small and narrow spots. Plastic erasers work very well as they don't lift the ink from your paper.

PRACTiCE!!! No professional artist gets to the stage they're at without practicing.

QUiCK TiP!

Ink

After the picture is drawn, artists will often outline their work and paint in shadows with black Indian ink. This inking stage is important if you're making a finished piece because it makes the lines bolder and more suitable for print.

If you look through existing manga you'll see that every panel is inked, giving the impression pencils were never used in the first place.

There are three tools you can use to apply ink to a picture – a pen and nib, a paintbrush or a marker pen.

Many artists have days when they hate inking, but they do anyway. Use India ink not only because it dries fairly quickly, but also because it is waterproof. An effective way to ink is to keep your strokes in the same direction and work as swiftly as possible. This way you will reduce the likelihood of unwelcome drips, splodges and wrinkles. And using a blow dryer on your illustration also reduces wrinkles!

Advantages

① Inking a picture finalizes and strengthens a line to make the image bold and ready for any coloring that may take place.

② Using varied line widths will make the picture appear dynamic and can give a 3D effect.

Disadvantages

① Ink is permanent so whatever you put on paper will stay there and cannot be removed without spoiling your paper and drawing! Successful inking is a skilled process and requires a different technique to pencilling. Practice by inking several sketches before applying ink to your finished piece, just to get used to the medium.

Watercolor

With the pencilling complete, watercolor painting provides subtle tones and delicate pastel washes. Your drawing will have a loose and fluid feel rather than the bold and graphical effect you get with inking. Watercolors are very organic in the way they are applied and appear on the paper, and suit a fine-art style of working.

One renowned manga artist that uses such coloring regularly is Masamune Shirow. Although Shirow's early work was painted with traditional brushes, he has embraced computer technology and now does most of his coloring digitally.

Both methods are viable but working digitally gives you more control over the medium.

Advantages

① Delicate washes can be used. These usually indicate femininity

② Watercolor is quick and easy to apply.

Disadvantages

① It is an unusual technique for manga and takes practice to look effective. As it's rarely used throughout a manga comic book it's best suited to a stand-alone piece of work.

② Ordinary drawing paper is not suitable for watercolor painting. You need thicker paper for the paints to be absorbed effectively without running.

Rulers

Try to use your rulers as little as possible and practice drawing straight and curved lines without them. In the end the only thing you'll need your ruler for is drawing frames or borders on a comic, or for helping when cutting out your illustration. However, as you will no doubt use them initially here's a quick tip – those of you who have tried inking may have noticed that the ink tends to bleed/smear if you aren't careful. The easiest way to avoid this is to use a ruler with an elevated edge. You can elevate your ruler by taping a coin (about the size of a quarter) to the underside. It works really well!

Celluloids with Acrylic

Acetate is the thin plastic sheet that pictures are painted on for use in animation. When the acetate has an image on it, it is referred to as a Celluloid, or Cel for short. If you're keen on painting and using color, making cels might appeal. Although most manga is black and white, cel works are always in color and you can create manga images in the style of your favorite anime! Much of the art in this book lends itself well to the anime style so why not give it a try?

Acetate sheets are available from good art shops and come in various sizes and thickness and are affordable, much like paper. The size of the sheets used in professional productions is 10.3" x 9" for 4:3 ratio series or 13" x 9" for widescreen presentations. However, if you're planning to make individual pictures just choose whichever size you please. To create a background for your cel you can paint with watercolors on a sheet of cartridge paper.

Advantages

① Painting on to acetate is the best way to emulate the 'anime look' – it's the way in which real cel animation is made.

② Once the outline is drawn on to the cel, it's easy to fill in the gaps with flat color.

Disadvantages

① Take care when handling acetate by wearing cotton gloves; even the cleanest fingers leave natural oils, which slightly mark the surface.

② Painting in reverse may be a little confusing at first.

Digital Art

Computers are now greatly exploited as software/hardware becomes more advanced, cheaper and readily available to home users. Digital art can facilitate and combine drawing, inking and coloring all in one. You can draw effectively via the computer using a Graphics Tablet, and inking and coloring can be achieved through a variety of software packages. Digital artwork is vitally important in manga artwork.

Advantages

① Paper, pencils, pens and other traditional tools are not required.

② Mistakes can be erased or altered easily.

③ Different techniques and effects can be used to enhance the image – there are few limitations to what you can achieve with a still image.

Disadvantages

① Buying a computer with the necessary hardware and software is very expensive but it becomes cost effective if you get a lot of use from it.

② The final product only exists in a 'virtual world' – printing your work isn't as tactile as traditional artwork methods.

Other Tools

Of course there are other tools and materials available to aid your creativity, which can be just as important. Items such as paper, templates and a light box can help you achieve effective results. Not forgetting your workspace, which should be kept clean and tidy with everything to hand.

Work Area

Keep it clean and lean like a well-oiled machine. Poor rhyming aside, your workstation is vital to producing good illustrations. You must be comfortable (get a decent chair!) and have everything you need easily to hand. Avoid clutter, and ensure the area is well lit. You may also want to keep a number of books and other reference materials close to hand for quick and easy inspiration or guidance!

ADS

It's the initial focus of your manga character and the first thing you'll start drawing – the head is key to your creation. There are two main areas that drawing the head can help you define: proportion and pose. If you flick through this book you'll see a particular style to the artwork which is typical of most manga – a standard body-sized representation. Other styles include Chibi (child bodied) and Super Deform, abbreviated to SD (simplified miniature creations).

The head can be used as a tool to measure the proportions of the whole body so sketching this correctly is the first step to a competent looking drawing. More information on this can be found within the 'Body' section but let's not get ahead of ourselves!

By itself, a head doesn't look like much. Only when the facial features are added does it begin to take on personality. However, you'll want to make the character appear dynamic and this is largely achieved by the pose, not only of the character's body but also the angle of the head.

When starting off, it's good to start practicing a lot of front view angles to get the style and facial features correct, then move on to an angle of the head and a side/profile angle, all of which have been illustrated in this section.

Good luck!

HEADS

Drawing the head (and the face that fits it!) is one of the most important, and often daunting, tasks of a manga character illustration. In this section there are a number of step-by-step examples to help you become a confident constructor of craniums, but to begin with, always bear these points in mind:

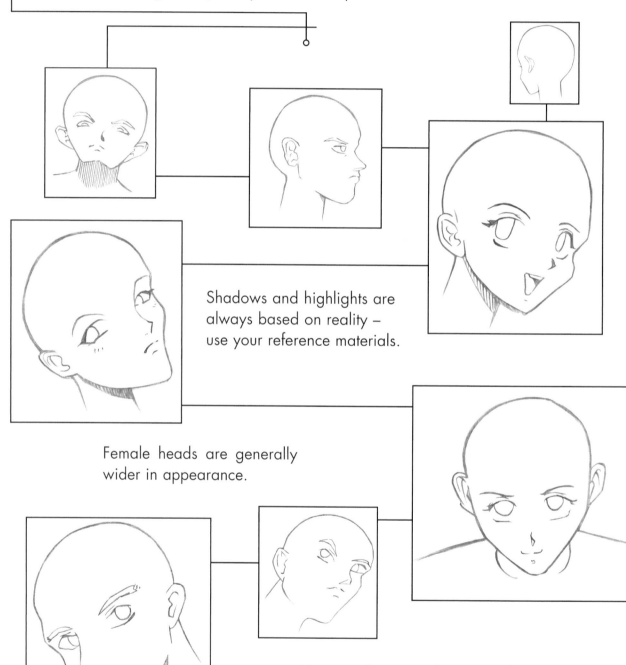

Shadows and highlights are always based on reality – use your reference materials.

Female heads are generally wider in appearance.

Younger characters have 'circular' shaped heads with bigger eyes and smaller noses than their adult counterparts.

The shape of the head and facial features differ depending on age and personality.

Female eyes are always drawn bigger to make them look more appealing.

Always keep your guide lines tight – they aren't part of the final illustration but are essential to aid proportion and symmetry.

Press lightly or use lighter pencils when drafting out your head illustration so mistakes can be erased easily.

STEP 1 ▶

All heads can start from drawing a circle with a center line. It is not necessary to draw a perfect circle. Note that these lines are guide lines and are not all supposed to be left on your final drawing so remember to draw them lightly so that they can be erased later.

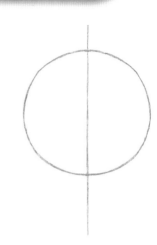

◀ STEP 2

Male faces are generally longer and more angular than female faces. Draw two parallel vertical lines downward from the side edges of the circle. Slope the lines inwards to create the jaw.

STEP 3 ▶

Fill out the proportions of the face by adding guide lines. Near the bottom of the circle you can see the eye and eyebrow lines which are spaced equally apart. Mark in where the beginning and end of each eye goes. Remember to keep things symmetrical by using the center guide line to help. Draw a square down from the center of the bottom of the circle. The bottom of this square will be where the nose ends. Draw two equally spaced horizontal guides below the square – these are the lip guides. I've also marked in where the bottoms of the ears go – just above the slope of the jaw.

◀ STEP 4

Add in some facial details – eyeballs, eyebrows and nose. The nose is represented by shadow – this is right of the center line. Draw boxes for where the ears will go – the top of the boxes are just above the eyebrow. Neck lines should fall parallel from the jaw. The neck should be just a bit narrower than the width of the head. Draw in the hairline on the forehead.

STEP 5 ▸

Define the eyes inside the guide boxes. The nose shadow line goes up to the bottom of the circle. The mouth and bottom lip are added, then guide lines removed. Add detailing to the inside of the ears and provide a rough idea of where the hair will go. Hair can't grow from below the hairline. Put lines where the neck tendons are.

STEP 6 ▴

Add finishing details and solidify your final lines – erase guide lines and clean up the image.

Now it's all ready to color!

Look at magazines, manga and comics for reference to see how the pros do it. As soon as you understand what makes an anime style and why artists draw the way they do, it makes the learning process easier.

QUICK TIP!

STEP 1 ▶

Start with a circle. Because the head is at an angle the center line curves and is aligned towards the way the head will be facing – left. The bottom chin line is drawn at a slant.

◀ STEP 2

On the left draw the cheek bone as a diagonal line extending from the circle. Join this to the bottom of the jaw. Draw the cheek bone and jaw line as shown on the diagram.

STEP 3 ▶

Draw eye lines parallel to the chin. The top eye line joins where the circle meets the cheek line.

◀ STEP 4

Extend the line down from center line to the corner of the guide box to create the nose. Create a box for the ear. The first neck line comes down from near the center of the chin, the second comes down from the ear.

STEP 5 ▶

Add details to the eyes, mouth and ears. Rough out where hair will go and remove the guide lines.

STEP 6 ▲

Add finishing details and solidify your final lines. Erase guide lines and clean up the image.

Now it's all ready to color!

STEP 1 ▶

Start by drawing a circle – it doesn't have to be perfectly round. Intersect the circle with two lines towards the bottom right area, one line horizontal, the other vertical. These are guide lines so should be drawn in lightly so they can be erased later.

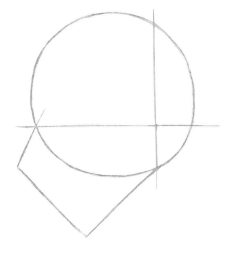

◀ STEP 2

Draw a box diagonally starting from where the intersect guides meet the bottom of the circle. This box is the jaw line guide.

STEP 3 ▶

Add eye line guides – the top guide runs horizontal and parallel to the existing intersect line. Add in the eye, which is triangle-shaped. Add guides for the bottom of the nose, mouth and bottom lip. Also note where the bottom of the ear starts.

◀ STEP 4

Add in some facial details such as the eyeball and eyebrow. Begin a vertical guide, and box in the ear. The biggest step is to chisel out the mouth and chin. Add in the neck lines and indicate where the top of the hair line is.

STEP 5 ▶

Add more facial details and round off the mouth, lips and chin. Rough out where the hair will be. Hair will grow from above the hairline guide. Add a neck tendon in a diagonal line.

STEP 6 ▲

Add finishing details and solidify your final lines. Erase guide lines and clean up the image.

Now it's all ready to color!

STEP 1 ▶

Remember all heads can start from drawing a circle with a center line. It is not necessary to draw a perfect circle. As before, remember to draw guide lines lightly so that they can be erased later.

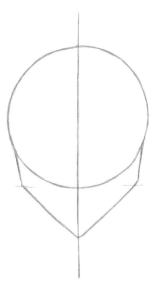

◀ STEP 2

Female faces are generally rounder, smaller and a lot less angular than male faces. Draw two short parallel vertical lines downward from the side edges of the circle. Slope the lines inwards sharply to create a smaller jaw.

STEP 3 ▶

Fill out the proportions of the face by adding more guide lines. Mark in where each eye goes – note these will be bigger than male eyes. Remember to keep things symmetrical by using the center guide line to help. Draw a square down from the center of the bottom of the circle. This square will form the mouth.

◀ STEP 4

Add in some facial details. As you would expect, features such as the nose should be a lot less prominent. Draw in the outline of the ears – they will help you shape the hair at a later stage. Neck lines should fall parallel from the jaw and equidistant from the center line. The neck should be just a bit narrower than the width of the head. Draw in a small 'v' to mark the hairline on the forehead.

STEP 5 ▶

Define the eyes inside the guide boxes. The eyes should be big and bold as this is a strong feature of many manga female characters. Add detailing to the inside of the ears and begin to sketch in the hair around the form of the face. Turn the neck lines into a curved shape to suggest a more graceful, female form.

STEP 6 ▲

Add finishing details and solidify your final lines. Put lots of life into the eyes by carefully shading the pupils. These are your character's most prominent feature so work hard to get it right. Erase guide lines and clean up the image.

Now it's all ready to color!

STEP 1 ▶

Start with a circle. Because the head is at an angle the center line curves and is aligned towards the way the head will be facing – left. The bottom chin line is drawn at a slant.

◀ STEP 2

On the left draw the cheek bone as a diagonal line extending from the circle. Join this to the bottom of the jaw/chin. Draw the cheek bone and jaw line as shown on the diagram.

STEP 3 ▶

Parallel to the chin draw eye lines. The top eye line meets where the circle meets the cheek line.

◀ STEP 4

Extend the line down from the center line to the corner of the guide box for the nose. Create a box for the ear. The first neck line comes down from near the center of the chin, the second comes down from the ear.

STEP 5 ▶

Add details to eyes, mouth and ears. Rough out where the hair will go. Remove guide lines.

STEP 6 ▲

Add the finishing details and solidify your final lines. Erase guide lines and clean up the image.

Now it's all ready to color.

STEP 1 ▶

Start by drawing a circle. It doesn't have to be perfectly round. Intersect the circle with two lines towards the bottom right area, one line horizontal, the other vertical. These are guide lines so should be drawn in lightly so they can later be erased.

◀ STEP 2

Draw a box diagonally starting from where the intersect guides meet the bottom of the circle. This box is the jaw line guide.

STEP 3 ▶

Add eye line guides – the top guide runs horizontal and parallel to the existing intersect line. Add in the eye, which is triangle-shaped. Equally space horizontal lines. Add as guides for the bottom of the nose, mouth and bottom lip. Also add in at the point where the bottom of the ear starts.

◀ STEP 4

Add in some facial details – eyeball and eyebrow. Begin vertical guide, box in the ear. Biggest step is to chisel out the mouth and chin. Add in the neck lines. Add where the top of the hair line is.

STEP 5 ▶

Define more facial details – eye, eyebrow, inside of ear. Round off the mouth, lips and chin. Rough out where the hair will be. Hair will grow from above the hairline guide. Add the neck tendon with a diagonal line.

STEP 6 ▲

Add finishing details and solidify your final lines. Erase guide lines and clean up the image.

Now it's all ready to color!

Do your drawings look a mess after constant erasing? Try pressing your pencil on the paper more lightly and use a pencil like a 2H. When you are happy with your work, you can go over the lines with a darker pencil (B) or ink.

QUICK TIP!

FAC

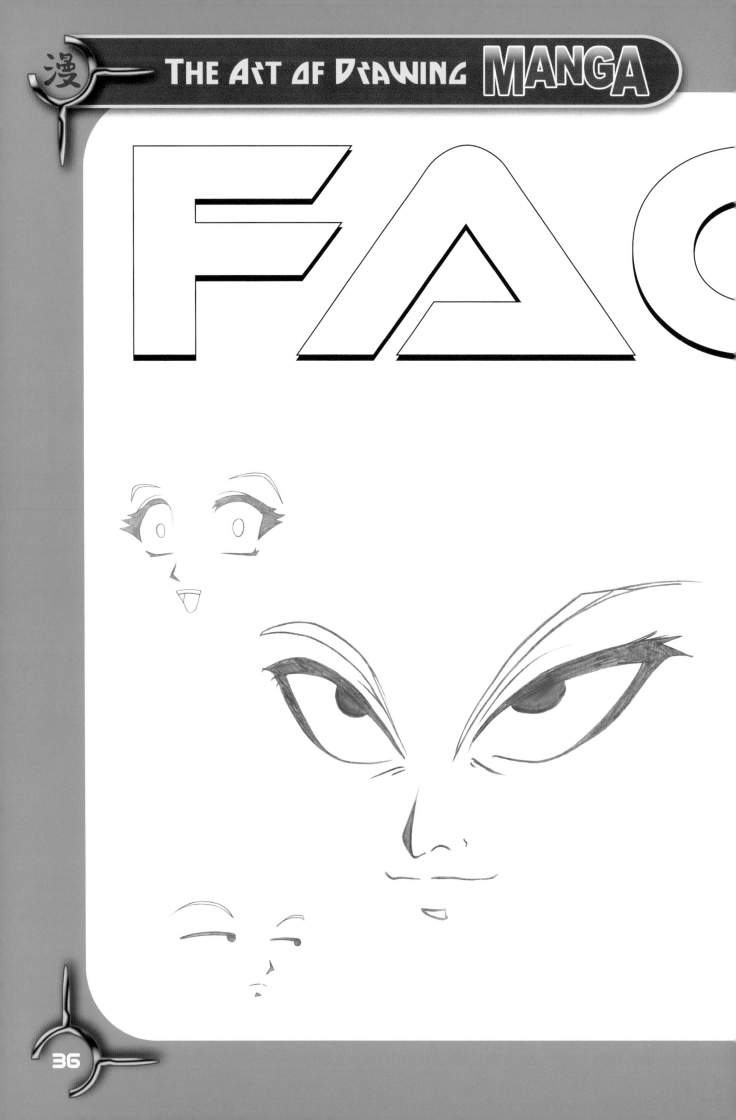

Once the head is drawn you naturally need to add a face and this is the really fun part! It is important to pay attention to detail here because the face will give your character personality and a lot will depend on the size and shape of the features. Drawing the face allows you to show whether a character is male or female, young or old, or even if they are good or evil.

When we see manga faces we can immediately tell them apart from real life portraits and other cartoon styles because of the particular techniques used to create them. Consider what you would have to think about when drawing a life-like picture of a person's face. There are a lot of details we see including the size and shape of features, bone structure and textures such as skin tone.

To 'animize' a face we use a degree of simplification and suggestion – this is true for all cartoon styles but the application is unique in manga.

Manga faces are often idyllic and beautiful; they will have a flat, smooth skin tone (wrinkles are only used to represent very old people) and simplified features. The eyes are often large and reflect a lot of light and the nose and mouth are represented with simple dashes or curves. As easy as this might sound, there are right and wrong ways to draw features which are outlined in this section.

EYES

It's time to get going on the face and I'll begin with the eyes, which I think are the hardest part to master. The hair comes a close second!

Why is drawing eyes the hardest to master? Primarily because the eyes play such an important role in expressing the character of your creation. Not only do you have to make sure that the eyes are balanced, you also have to draw the eyes so that they show the emotion of the character. Hair might be difficult to draw, but mastering it isn't hard when compared to eyes.

There are many different types of eyes (and eyebrows!), and I've included a few examples to give you some ideas. Eyes can take many different shapes and sizes, and they may appear fairly easy to draw – they are, but only badly!

Looking at the range of samples I've provided, do you think you can easily spot the different male and female eyes?

'*Jagged*' eyebrows are used for characters that have an exceptional or exaggerated personality. Many villains have these eyebrows, but you very rarely see them used for female characters!

'*Streamlined*' eyebrows are the most commonly used. They can be a straight line, a 'hill', or a small wave.

When drawing male eyes, male eyebrows are created, eyelashes are omitted, and the eyes are usually smaller than that of female characters.

Eyes can be hooded, wide open, or can glint in the light – they are vital to drawing character emotion.

These rules aren't written in stone as different characters have different personalities and you'll need to break the rules occasionally. For example a strong, adventurous woman may have thicker eyebrows.

Women tend to have thin eyebrows. The eyelashes are thicker and the eyes are bigger in comparison to a male.

◀ STEP 1

Some people prefer to start with a ball, but I think this approach produces a better eye. Begin by drawing a large off-center 'V' and somewhere around the middle draw two opposing curved lines. This represents the orb of the eye and helps with the general placement of the eye in the skull.

STEP 2 ▶

Here's where most budding artists can go wrong. The lids wrap around the contour of the orb. Imagine stretching a sheet of rubber over a cue ball. The eyelid hugs the curvature of the eye.

◀ STEP 3

The eye in a relaxed state hides some of the iris behind the lids. Notice how the iris takes up most of the surface area of the orb. This really only occurs in manga. Also sketch in your eyebrow – as you may have already guessed this is a female eye so the eyebrow is thin. You've now got the basics of your eye in place.

STEP 4 ▶

It now starts getting more complex as you add the details that will set your eyes apart from other illustrators! Have a look at the shapes I've sketched in – they won't make much sense at the moment but all will be revealed as we start to color the eye in. This is all about the reflection of light and the role of shadows.

STEP 5 ▶

Up until now the eye has been fairly plain. Flesh out the eyelids with some heavy duty, fluttering lashes. This adds weight to the eye so it's not simply floating around on the face. It also draws the viewer's attention. The thickness of the lashes will depend on the character you are creating. Obviously male characters won't have this trait and younger females should also have a thinner line. This eye is more for the sexy adult female. Also note the small 'x' in certain areas – this is to denote where I'm going to add solid color.

◀ STEP 6

A 'specular' is the reflection of light on a reflective surface. The placement of the specular on the eye should be indicative of the local light source. If the light is coming from the upper left the specular should be on the upper left of the iris. In this case the light enters the eye from the upper left and exists through the lower right. In manga speculars are also used to add emotion to the character. For example, sparkling light brings life to happy eyes.

Here's the finished eye – better get on with the other one!

NOSES & MOUTHS

Manga style noses and mouths are pretty straightforward, so rather than taking you through various types step-by-step, I have included a number of examples to give you an idea of the styles you can use.

The basic style nose and mouth consists of three simple steps: a wedge for the nose, a long, thin line for the mouth, and a shorter line to define the lower lip (although this lower line is not always included). With frontal views you can get away with using very few lines to define the nose and mouth. The size and shape of each feature varies with each character.

The main thing to consider is the curve of the nose, lips, and chin. The upper lip curves inward, and lower lip curves outward.

Female characters will tend to have smaller, less defined noses, while male characters will often have longer, angular noses.

Even though the proportions and expressions can change, most noses and mouths stick to the same basic shapes.

However, it may take some practice before your character doesn't look like they're making a weird face or puckering their lips!

Manga mouths are not often very large, unless the character is yelling or shouting, so keep them relatively small.

When drawing faces in profile, try not to make the noses really pointy and the face too flat. Make sure the features curve properly, or the face is going to look slightly strange.

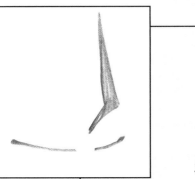

Several of the examples here can be used for either gender. Notice that with some styles, only a thin, straight line defines the mouth.

FACES

EXPRESSIONS

EXPRESSIONS

This is all pretty much self-explanatory – you put an expression on a face to give the viewer as clear an idea as possible of the emotion your character is expressing or experiencing.

On the following pages you will find a number of expressions that will cover most of the basic emotions your characters are likely to feel. Try drawing the expressions one by one – you'll soon get a feel for placement of the various features and how different expressions radically change your character's look!

‹ Angry

This is the face of someone who is really, really mad! The eyebrows come down sharply, the pupils shrink and you get a pulsing vein on the forehead. Fanged teeth help convey the emotion!

Annoyed ›

The pupils are still small but there are no popping veins or fanged teeth! The mouth goes up in an upside down lopsided 'u'. The eyebrows are still down but not as far.

‹ Evil

One of my favorites! The eyebrows are drawn thinly and look sharp – they point downwards. Dark eyelids obscure the iris and pupils giving a hooded look. The nose is small and pointed and the mouth is thin and slightly upturned at each corner – suggesting a sly smile.

Friendly ▸

The eyebrows are up. A thin line follows the upper curve of the eye to convey a relaxed state. The mouth is a sideways 'D'.

◂ Happy

The eyes shut from laughing or smiling. The mouth is in huge sideways 'D' mode and the eyebrows are up. You could even add some blush to the cheeks if you wanted to make really sure everyone knows your character is happy.

Sad ▸

The eyebrows are up, the mouth is a down-turned line and the open eyes have more sparkles in them to convey a wet look. Tears are visible in the corners of the eye.

◂ Surprise

The eyebrows are UP! The eyes are very wide open but the pupils are small. The mouth takes the form of a sort of lopsided 'O'.

Having trouble with drawing faces and expressions? Try keeping a little mirror with you when you draw. Just pull the type of face you're after and draw what you see!

QUICK TIP!

HAIR

Hair can be particularly difficult to draw, but unfortunately it's just something that takes practice and cannot be taught with a simple step-by-step. The different styles are just too numerous to cover in this book!

Depending on the style, manga hair can be very complex. However, if you break it down into its basic components, the process of drawing manga hair becomes a little simpler.

Like real hair, manga hair is composed of many strands. However, rather than drawing each individual strand, the hair is often drawn in various sized/shaped clumps.

You can either make the hair very detailed, or very simple, depending on how many individual strands you draw.

You can make some really interesting hair by having it twist and turn all over the page.

Keep in mind that you can make the hair as detailed as you like; just keep adding more strands.

Once you know how to draw each strand/clump of hair, you can start putting them together to form something that closely resembles anime hair.

The same similar shapes generally persist throughout many different hairstyles. Making one line curve out more than the other on each strand can really help to flesh it out.

The size and shape of each strand gives the hair different character; the strands can be long and thin, thick and curvy, or sharp and spiky.

Here, I will be talking about drawing hands. Hands are absolutely vital to the overall look of your finished artwork. So many people treat them as an afterthought and yet think about how much you use your hands every single day. So take your time to get the basics right to insure the hands are every bit as good as the other aspects of your character studies.

The basic form and procedure for constructing hands is similar to that of figure drawing. You break the overall shape down to simpler sizes, and then connect them all together. With good composition, you can draw hands from any angle possible.

When drawing hands, try not to think of the detailed contours, but rather the composition of the hand structure broken down in simpler terms. And remember how many different aspects there are to a hand – in effect it's a torso with five limbs!

It can also take on many different shapes and forms, all adding particular aspects to your character and the overall composition. A clenched fist, a wave, a thumbs-up – they all project very different stories and are vital to enforcing the image of your character's actions.

However, if you're still struggling with the complexities of hands after going through the advice in this section, don't panic! The great aspect of manga is that you are encouraged to be creative with your drawings. If you can't draw a human hand then make it something else!!!

HANDS

Hands can be a nightmare for most artists. It's hard to construct a hand in basic shapes so instead break it up into major forms and really pay attention to where it folds and bends.

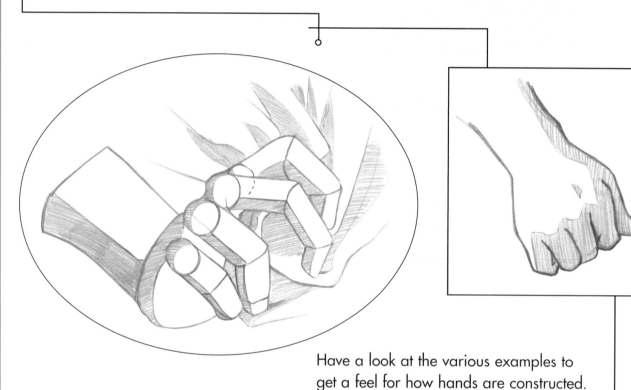

Have a look at the various examples to get a feel for how hands are constructed.

The hand is a bit like a shovel. The palm gives you the lines you need to see where it bends.

The thumb side of the palm pivots from the center.

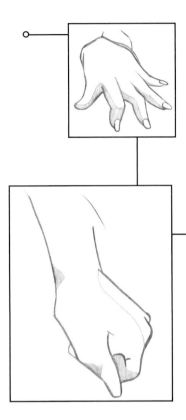

Never make the hand a flat wedge. It curves and follows the contours of the lines on the palm.

It is essential to recognize how the joints in the fingers and wrist work if you are to draw an accurate representation of a hand in action.

Even when drawing the hand from the back, pay attention to the fold lines in the palm. It will help you draw more natural positions for the thumb and fingers.

Notice how shading is vital in highlighting the actions the hands are carrying out.

◀ STEP 1

Start with a very simple orb. Make sure it doesn't take up too much of the paper as you need to draw quite a lot around it. I know it seems strange starting with a circle but trust me, it'll all come together!

STEP 2 ▶

Now draw a gently curving line across the bottom half of the orb – this will provide a guide to the middle of the outstretched palm. Also add a simple curve around three quarters of the orb – this marks the end of the fingers.

◀ STEP 3

It's time to add the fingers and thumb, all as very simple tubes at this stage. As you can see, it's starting to look like a hand already! Notice how the thumb projects from the point where the palm line touches the circle.

STEP 4 ▶

Now it's beginning to look like a hand, you should start shaping the overall form. Take away your initial guidelines.

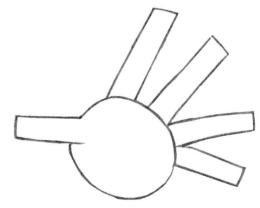

STEP 5 ▶

Round off the fingers and thumb at both ends. You now have fingers with tips but also a clear indication of where the fingers and thumb join the palm. Square off the original circle to give the hand its recognizable flatter, more angular shape.

◀ STEP 6

Put in all the details to really bring your hand to life. The best way to do this is obviously to look at your own hand. Note the use of simple lines to create effective wrinkles and creases, all adding to the realistic look of the hand.

STEP 7 ▶

The color puts the icing on the cake. Use careful but simple shading to bring out the tones of the hand and emphasize its position and action.

FIGU

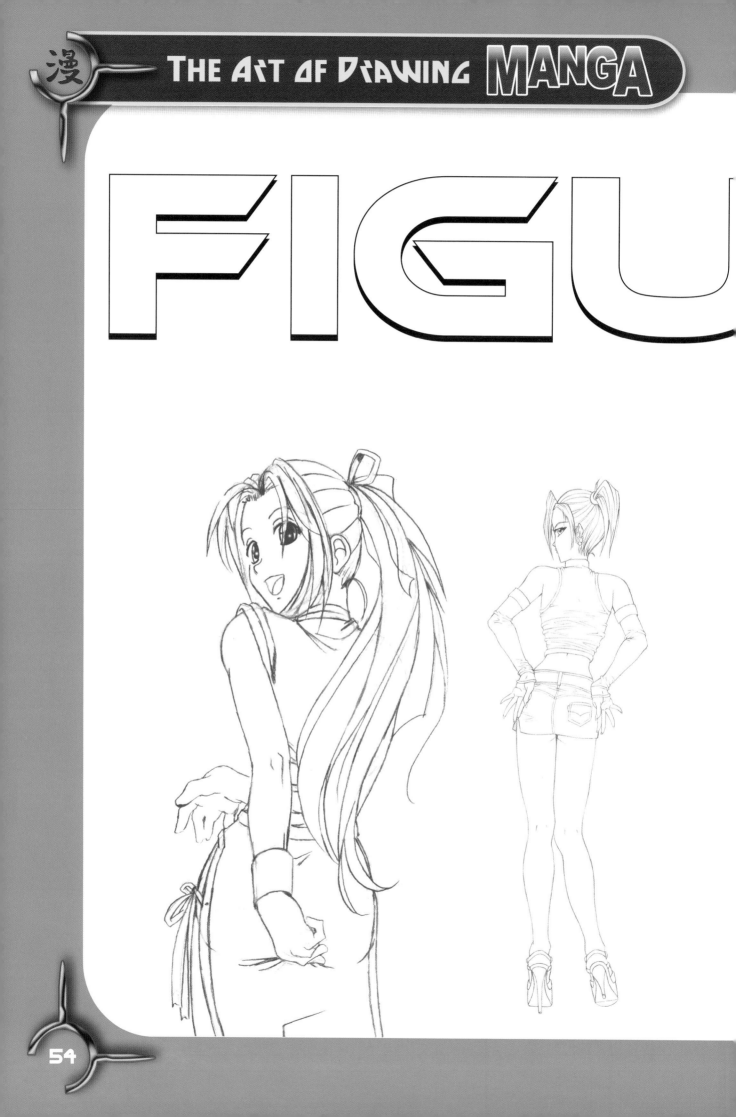

RES

Having looked at constructing the head and face we can begin to address the body. Again, it is a very important stage where we define the character's appearance in terms of size and muscle structure, their proportions, and also apply your chosen style.

What are the differences between manga proportions and real-life proportions? Many 'animanga' characters, especially the focal heroes, are teenagers/young adults – the reason is because this media is largely marketed to the age group that identifies with them the most. Such characters are often slim and athletic with longer legs than real-life people.

The character's pose is depicted by the body and is one of the most descriptive parts of the picture. Think about the angles you could use to make the picture visually interesting and what body language you can suggest to help explain a character's actions and movement. You should think of yourself as a film director who chooses the camera angles and tells the actors how you want them to move and act in a situation. This is an analogy worth using again when we come to look at creating manga layouts and panels.

Whether someone is in a dynamic action shot or slouching in a chair, it has a direct effect on the composition of the picture and gives us information about that character's actions, personality and the overall mood of the scene. Don't think too deeply about the construction of your picture, these are just considerations that should be in the back of your mind – after some practice you'll come up with ingenious ideas on how to get the most from poses.

BASIC SHAPES

Look at the shapes below. Seem simple huh? Well practice them until you can't draw anymore, and then practice some more, because these shapes form the cornerstone of all the figure work you are ever likely to do in manga. Whenever you're bored, doodle these shapes and practice shading and developing them, maybe linking the shapes together. Over the next few pages you'll discover just why they are so important.

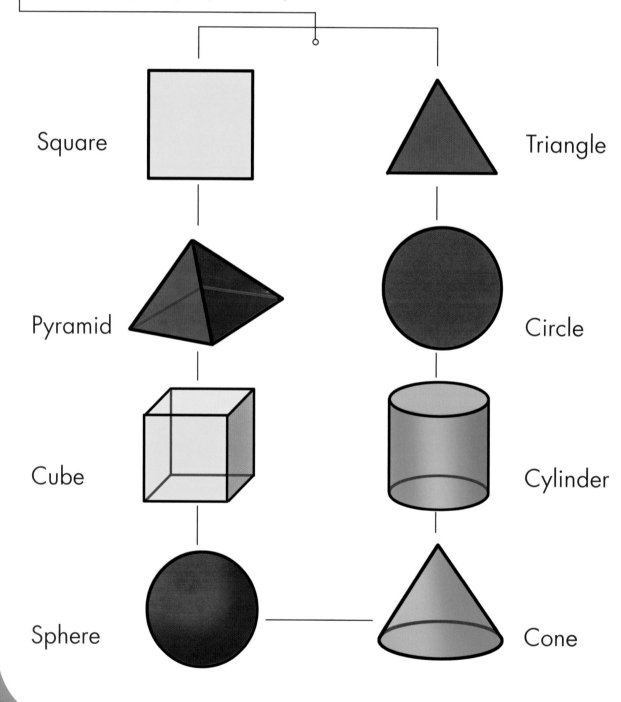

Square

Triangle

Pyramid

Circle

Cube

Cylinder

Sphere

Cone

PROPORTIONS

Average Manga Proportions:
Note: The body is proportioned to the size of the eyes and head.

Body Height
6.5 - 7.5 head heights high.

Head
3.5 eye heights high by 4 - 4.5 eye widths wide.

Eyes
a little more than one eye width apart.

Mouth
about one eye height above the chin.

Neck
three eye widths wide.

Shoulders
twice as wide as the head, one eye height below the chin.

Upper Arm
slightly less than the width of the neck – the distance from elbow to armpit is one head height.

Lower Arm
distance from wrist to elbow is slightly more than one head height (same as length of foot).

Hand
about ¾ head height long.

Chest/High Bust
same width as height of head (distance between armpits).

Bust
fullest point falls one head height below the chin. Breasts are three eye widths wide.

Waist
falls one eye height below elbow, slightly less than width of the chest.

Hips
1¾ - 2 times the width of the head.

Legs
about half of overall height.

Upper leg (thigh)
almost as wide as head.

Knee
two head heights above the bottom of the foot.

Lower leg (calf)
same as neck.

Foot
length is slightly more than height of head.

These average proportions will work for a male or female character. But, for a male character, you may wish to expand the width of the chest slightly and make the hips 1¾ width of the head. For a female, keep the width of the chest the same as the height of the head but make the hips two head widths wide.

STEP 1 ▶

All right, now that we've gone over some of the major areas in detail, let's put them all together and make a full body pose. When drawing your subject, you can either begin with the preliminary ovals and circles, or you can go straight to the final draft, whichever you are most comfortable with. If you are using circles and ovals, then you will notice that the main body (torso and pelvis) is composed of a basic triangular shape, which curves inwards towards the stomach.

◀ STEP 2

Make sure that this shape is aligned along the central guide line (as shown in the head). This guide line in the head can basically be continued to form the spine of the character, and will determine the pose she is going to be in. Notice here that the center line curves to the right a little on the pelvis; this is because her weight is shifted and her right hip sticks out slightly (which makes the pose a little more interesting than if her weight is evenly balanced).

STEP 3 ▶

The body can be equally divided in half if the center line in the head is continued down the body. You can use that as a general reference when determining how long the legs should be in proportion to the rest of the body, but often in manga the length of the legs is exaggerated for both males and females, and it looks just fine. When drawing the midsection, remember to try to keep the hourglass figure shape.

◀ STEP 4

Female manga characters will generally have thin shoulders, a thin stomach, and a somewhat round waist. Be careful to make the curves look natural, unless you are really good at figure drawing and can exaggerate the proportions. Begin adding clothes (as many or as little as you like) to cover up the areas that can be particularly hard to draw. It is very difficult to draw the female chest for example so use clothing to make this easier and hide any parts of the figure you are not happy with.

STEP 5 ▶

It's time to fill in all the details. Add nails to the fingers, fill in the eyes and ears, and think carefully about creases and shading on the clothes.

◀ STEP 6

Remember to make the eyes big and almond shaped. Notice how adding eyelashes opens up the eyes even more, and helps accentuate the femininity of the face.

◀ **STEP 7**

You're now ready to use color. Remember to keep it simple for maximum effect! You've now created your first female figure.

STEP 1 ▸

Start building your figure using basic shapes. Look at the arms – the arms consist of three basic sections: the upper arm, the forearm, and the hand. Each can be represented in preliminary sketches by oval shapes. Now, I know some people don't like using the shapes; you do not have to do it this way, this is just one possible way to go about sketching arms.

◂ STEP 2

Some recommend using cylinders, but it's better to use flat ovals because they more closely match the shape of the arm. If the arms are held loosely at the side as here, the hands should come down to the middle of the thigh. The elbows should be at about waist length.

STEP 3 ▸

Draw in some hair and add the outlines of the costume. Note how the male figure does not have sloping shoulders like female characters. The body tends to be made up of solid blocks or slabs of shape rather than smaller, curved shapes. By drawing the hands as clenched fists you can suggest strength and power in the pose.

STEP 4 ▶

It's time to give your figure drawing some life. Start adding the smaller details. Notice how the ripples and creases you put in the clothes can help define the idea of the muscles underneath (without actually having to draw them).

◀ STEP 5

Remember to keep the lines and detailing simple, but notice that small details can add a great deal, such as giving your character stubble or a slight frown by angling the eyebrows downwards.

Learn to draw realistically – once you've gained some proficiency in that then try manga style. It's much easier to stylize once you know anatomy basics and understand why you're stylizing something.

QUICK TIP!

◀ STEP 6

The coloring stage can often make or break your figure drawing. Use careful shading to accentuate body parts (e.g. biceps) and to highlight individual aspects, such as hair or eyes. Often color can be used to draw attention to character aspects that are hard to highlight with just a sketch. You could, for example, match hair color with aspects of the clothes to build up a stronger overall image.

STEP 1 ▶

Try using a different method to structure your figure this time. Instead of ovals and other shapes, let's construct the figure using simple curved lines, with dots highlighting the figure's joints. It looks a bit like a join the dots picture!

◀ STEP 2

This technique essentially stems from stick people doodles that we've all put together at some point or other. The emphasis is on keeping it simple, but think carefully about where the joints are as they help construct an accurate pose for your figure.

STEP 3 ▸

Now build up some bones around the original lines and dots. Before long you'll end up with a figure that starts to resemble a human skeleton.

◂ STEP 4

You'll notice the pose still looks slightly awkward at this stage, and the figure is still robotic looking rather than human.

STEP 5 ▶

Look out for the neck at this angle; it connects up into the skull, and should be obscured by part of the face.

The midsection should be somewhat hourglass shaped, but again, don't over-exaggerate the curve unless you really know your anatomy (you have to know the basics before you can start bending the rules). Don't over-define the lines on the behind, since there's little reason to.

Be careful when drawing the arms; from the back, the elbows should be more prominent than usual.

◀ STEP 6

Now you've got some flesh on the bones take out your original guide lines and start building in more details. Notice how very small, but simple, curved lines help give a suggestion of how your figure is posed, such as the curved lines on the back of the knees and the slight arch in the back.

Experiment with as many varieties of media as possible. Chances are you'll find something you like beyond your pencil.

QUICK TIP!

◂ STEP 7

Add some very basic blocks of color. Feel free to stop at this stage if you want to – your figure is perfectly formed. However, if you really want to go to town…

SUMMERTIME

STEP 8 ▶

...then you can use color to really emphasize the pose of your figure and even suggest aspects of the backdrop. This all adds character and life to your drawing.

STEP 1 ▶

Remember all those stick people you used to draw in school – this is where you realize how useful they were. Begin with a loose stick figure that will serve as your foundation. Note that the form is about 7 heads high. Notice that you can draw a line straight up and down from the top of the head to the bottom of the feet. Body mass is distributed equally on both sides of this axis for balance.

◀ STEP 2

In manga the legs are made to look slightly longer than the upper half of the body. The knees are located halfway between the top of the hip and the bottom of the foot.

◀ STEP 3

The female torso can be given a casual yet sexy stance by slanting the shoulders and hips in different directions.

STEP 4 ▶

Now we start to flesh out
the illustration. You have to
be good at drawing
cylinders and ovals to do
this correctly. Study muscle
groups to get an idea of
how the shoulders, arms
and legs are formed. Try
to use only curved lines.
Nothing on a human being
is ruler-edge straight but
that holds especially true
for a female.
Curvy, curvy, curvy!

◀ STEP 4

Now start tightening up your
art. Grab a kneaded eraser
and start blotting away the
fine sketchy lines, keeping
only the lines you wish to
use for your final piece.
Getting your drawing clean
at this stage makes the next
stage that much easier.

STEP 5 ▶

Gradually start to complete the character by outlining the fleshed-out sketch from the last stage and smoothing over all the joints used to build the illustration. The eraser becomes very important at this point as you remove any stray lines and get a clean, usable piece of art.

◀ STEP 6

Start correcting mistakes made in the building process and get the line art as complete as possible, ready for inking. There's nothing worse than inking over sloppy pencil lines so make it as accurate as possible.

◄ **STEP 7**

...then you can use color to bring your character to life.

CLO1

Creating a character is not just about the figure; pay careful consideration to their clothing and accessories too. The clothing a character wears not only enhances their personality and gives us clues as to who they are, but it opens up a whole new doorway of drawing techniques. Whereas a body has standard forms and shapes, simplified to cylinders and circles, textiles come in many shapes, sizes, colors and textures.

We see clothing as a three-dimensional form through light reflected on its surface. This shows us folds and we can imagine what sort of texture a fabric might be by the shadows and highlights. Different fabrics reflect different amounts of light; leather is very reflective compared to tweed which absorbs light.

Have this in the back of your mind when you draw clothing to make it appear realistic. However, in manga, many of the costumes seem to defy gravity to an extent, such as billowing capes and tall hats that couldn't possibly exist in such a state in real life. This is where we can use some artistic license to make the character look dramatic and give the picture some added visual impact.
Try sketching several outfits over the frame of a character and play around with the designs each time to see how far you can go without making it look ridiculous.

It is important not to feel daunted. In manga, you can simplify all these things and still achieve wonderful illustrations. On the following pages a few secrets will be revealed that will help you come up with some stunning results!

CLOTHING

I've included some examples of basic folds. Notice the movement in each of the examples. The fabric flows downward if pulled down by gravity, but folds become more horizontal than vertical the further they are stretched. Also notice how the folds are sometimes nested within one another. Folds follow the direction in which the cloth is being pulled.

Generally, you shade along a fold line, or on any places that you think a shadow would be cast.

It helps to look at actual folds to see where to shade.

As practice try sketching the drapes of a towel hung over a chair. You will start to get a better feel for how clothing is shaded.

Remember to use shading to give your subjects more form.

There are thousands of different styles of clothes, so rather than try to cover them all I thought it would be more useful to show you how clothes behave on the body. That way you can at least get the physics right and design whatever style of clothing you want.

When you first draw your character, don't worry about putting clothes on initially. Instead, make sure you have fleshed them out correctly. Clothes flow over the body like water. The folds on clothes are determined by kinetic force and gravity.

You have to imagine the way that the fabric will be pulled both by gravity and the motion of the wearer. Notice the clothing is smooth and taut over areas that are bent or push against the fabric. Fold lines radiate out and away from bends. Other areas of clothes in a more relaxed state succumb to gravity and fall downwards (e.g. the skirt).

Imagine small hoops around your arms, waist, neck and legs. If you raise your arm, how does the hoop hang? Which part of your arm is touching the hoop? The part that touches is where the clothing would outline your arm and the folds would radiate out and away from there. Clothes bunch up and hang in the opposite direction of the body's motion.

The most important thing to consider whenever you are drawing clothing or any type of fabric is the direction the fabric is going to be pulled in. Folds are caused wherever the fabric is being stretched or pulled; figure out how exactly you want the fabric to move, and the rest is pretty easy. Always remember to consider the figure beneath the clothing; the clothing should reveal the shape of the figure beneath.

Having trouble with clothes? You can buy realistic paper dolls featuring styles from every decade to traditional clothes from other cultures!

QUICK TIP!

ACCESS
& WEAP

SORIES
ONS

In addition to clothing, think about adding extra adornments to your character such as trinkets, personal artefacts and jewellery. Not only are these visually interesting, they also help promote the personality of your character, suggest events that occurred throughout their lifetime and give clues to their culture and background. Consider what adventures they may have been on and what souvenirs they might have picked up on their travels – a necklace, a bracelet, a ring or a hat are all favorites, but your ideas will depend upon the character's age, gender and the story setting (science fiction, medieval, school etc).

Another great way to emphasize a character's occupation or interests is to highlight 'tools of the trade'. For example, a computer hacker may be inseparable from her laptop, a spy may have an array of communication devices all over his body and most fantasy characters will have exotic weapons of some description.

In most modern and sci-fi comic book settings, guns and blades are often the weapons of choice, both because there is a style to them and they offer great destructive power. However, manga is firmly rooted in Japanese culture and tradition, and it's important to remember that through martial arts many everyday objects and farming tools were adapted to be used as weapons. The most common of traditional weapons are the Katana (sword), Bo (wooden staff) and Nunchaku (two wooden lengths attached by a length of chain).

For more ideas, put some research into this topic using magazines, books and the web so you can adapt various weapons for your own creations. Not only will this be rewarding but you'll also be creating original designs that will be appreciated by those who view your work.

ACCESSORIES & WEAPONS

The most important point to remember when creating accessories, whether clothes, weapons or jewellery, is to draw them with the necessary amount of detail. Be imaginative by all means but make the effort to fill in the details.

Yes, it is possible to draw the necklace by placing 6 circles next to one another, but does it look effective? Why go to all the effort of creating a visually stunning character but then rush the accessories?

You would think the buckle of a belt is simple but most people represent it as a square box on a thick line. A little attention to detail will make your illustration look sharper. Draw the buckle as shown here with the strap overlapping the back end of the buckle and with the thickness of the belt clearly visible.

Because of the nature of manga, weapons are often very important accessories for many characters, and you may want to include some with your own creations. Look at the two examples of a knife. With the use of foreshortening on the larger of the two examples you can create a very dynamic 'in your face' drawing – this adds a great deal of vibrancy and menace to your composition.

You might also want to consider the careful use of lensflares and shading to bring some realism and life to your accessories. Light glinting off a curved sword or twirling mace can radically increase the impact of your illustration.

Nothing helps with action drawing like good reference material. Get your friends to pose for you or clip pictures from magazines. Any time you see a pose you like, GRAB IT! You never know when you might need it. After a while you'll be able to draw from your imagination.

When choosing a pose for your character, think about his or her personality and how he or she moves. For instance, when walking, one character may strut along confidently while another may drag his feet and walk along with his head hung low. The mood you show depends on the pose, as well as the facial expression. Try to imagine how you stand or move in different moods.

The only way to get good at drawing action shots is to practice. In the following examples I've covered running, jumping, fighting and falling. Think of all the things you have learnt so far about figure drawing and clothing and bring them to bear on these examples.

The key here is the stick figure and the line of motion. Lots of artists get all caught up in the clothes and muscles and details way too early in the drawing. The key to a good action pose is a strong foundation and the stick figure will help us with that.

The first thing to draw is the line of motion. This line is a smooth curving line that runs from the top of the character's head, through the body via the spine and out. Build the stick figure on this line and flesh out the character around it.

Draw! Draw! Draw! Bored? Take out a piece of paper and doodle. Tired of watching TV? Draw that favorite anime character! When you draw every day, it makes a big difference!

QUICK TIP!

Here I've got a scary falling sequence going on. The character is waving his limbs and clearly dropping like a stone.
Concentrate on the shape and angles of the limbs to make the action believable and dynamic.

Use other features such as the hair, clothing and accessories to emphasize the speed of the fall. Everything pointing upwards suggests the wind is rushing past as gravity acts on the character.

STEP 1 ▶

The first key to drawing action poses is to go for broke. It's better to push the character too far than not enough. Go for poses that are dramatic, almost frightening! Action poses must also have a sweep to them, with the character traveling in a direction.

◀ STEP 2

This is as complicated as you should get when making a stick figure...stay fast and loose. Make little circles to show where the joints and head are. Don't worry about fingers and toes. Just make a solid stick person. Don't forget your line of action.

◀ STEP 3

The pose here is a prelude to another action. Clearly our character is going to descend on a target, using her aggression to either defend herself or attack someone else! You can clearly see the flow of the pose – it's a classic look with the arm raised above the head, adding huge drama to the illustration. The knees are tucked up, clearly showing your character has left the ground! The rest of the legs and torso are fairly straight. The raised arm also suggests a forward and downward motion.

STEP 4 ▸

You want to make it seem as if the character is bursting out of the picture, almost as if she's attacking the reader! You achieve this by making it appear that the figure is above the viewer, jumping down, ambush style! Notice how the character's clothing suggests a lot of movement. Even the frown of the eyebrows shows the character is making an aggressive downwards movement.

◀ STEP 1

Use your knowledge of creating figures to sketch out your runner. Notice how a curved or angled line of action can be used to pull your character towards the viewer. It can also be used to help exaggerate a position.

STEP 2 ▶

Here you see the use of some foreshortening in the pelvis and the shoulders because we are looking at the character slightly from the side. When running, the center of gravity lies in front of the resting point.

Before you do ink, try and relax your hands in some way – a shaky hand will leave the line art looking messy.

QUICK TIP!

STEP 3 ▶

As you can see, this is an unbalanced pose resulting in a falling motion of the figure. She won't fall of course, because she is running at speed and will put a foot in front of the other preventing her from hitting the ground.

STEP 4 ▶

The loosely flowing hair and the
folds in the character's clothes all
give the impression of movement.
Remember, it's not just body
shape alone that helps the viewer
interpret the character's actions.

With a fighting illustration you've got to make the picture as dynamic as possible if it is to have any effect on the viewer. Rough out your illustration using the tried and tested ovals and sticks. It doesn't look like much to begin with but already you can see the movement in the composition.

As you start to flesh in the two figures you can begin to see the dynamics of the punch. The force of the punch is shown in the shape and position of the characters. Choosing an angle that shows the moment of impact really pulls this action together.

Now THAT had to hurt! The use of foreshortening crumples the target's body. He probably won't be getting up for a while. Also, the attacker's body is very much a part of this punch – all the balance is thrown into it, giving the impression of a mighty delivery.

When you get to the stage of cleaning up your work and adding in details, be sure to incorporate lines that translate the action taking place. The edges of the fist and arm are quick strokes following the direction the arm is traveling. The head is knocked back from the point of impact.

Boooooom!

COLO

All great compositions partly owe their success to colors. Maybe you think the artist just needs to 'stay within the lines' and then they end up with a fantastic picture. Well, it's not as easy as that. Over the following pages you will find a selection of tips on getting the most from color, and valuable advice that will help you think before putting a single pixel of color in your drawing.

Okay, I know what you're saying: 'Come on! I know what red, blue or yellow looks like. I don't need you to tell me about it.' Maybe so. But remember, when you're out of ideas, always come back to the basics. You might learn something new!

Always remember that colors will create a certain atmosphere in your drawing. So think carefully what mood you want to give your work before starting with a color simply because it's your favorite. It doesn't work that way.

Color

Some useful terms that you should familiarize yourself with:

Hue

A pure color; the color itself (red, yellow, blue, etc).

Intensity

This refers to the brightness of a color. In order to lower a color's intensity (dull down), add a small amount of its complement; its opposite color (more about complements later). For example, to dull down red, add a bit of green. If equal amounts of red and green are mixed, the color becomes brown, not a dulled down red.

Value

This refers to the lightness or darkness of a color. For example, to lighten a color add white.

Primary Colors

Red, yellow, and blue. They are the basic colors that make up all the other colors of the color wheel. For example, if you mix red and yellow – you get the secondary color: orange. Mix red and blue – you get purple. Mix blue and yellow – you get green. And from there you can create tertiary colors like turquoise (a blue green color) or fuschia (a red purple color).

Secondary Colors

Orange, violet, and green. These are made mixing any of the primary colors as explained above.

Tertiary Colors

Colors made by mixing a primary and its secondary color.

Neutral Colors

When equal amounts of two complementary colors are used, a neutral gray or brown is made.

Color Moods

These are the basic moods:

Warm colors (red, orange) – suggest heat, energy, passion etc.

Cool colors (blue, green) – suggest cold, calm, relaxation etc.

Light colors (added white) – lightness, freedom, air, floating etc.

Dark colors (added black) – oppression, small, closed area etc.

Colorful (bright colors) – excitement, life, strong energy etc.

Before we get into the real coloring tips, it's worth bearing a question in mind. Have you ever experienced looking at your drawing and saying 'I can't stop looking at this or that but I don't know why!' The answer probably lies in the color. Look at the following list. It shows which colors are likely to make the most impact, from the one that gets most attention in a picture to the one that gets the least.

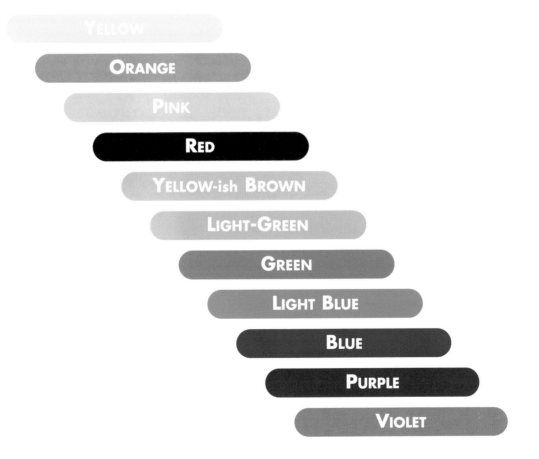

YELLOW

ORANGE

PINK

RED

YELLOW-ish BROWN

LIGHT-GREEN

GREEN

LIGHT BLUE

BLUE

PURPLE

VIOLET

So before you go crazy with colors, bear this in mind – the little yellow hat you give your character could gain far more attention than you wanted.
Be careful!!!!

Shadow and Shading

Shading can be a bit tricky at first but it's not as difficult as it seems. One side of a shape is light and the others are darkened. This is all you need to know when shading: what the light doesn't hit is darkened. Picture the light source and the object which is being hit by the light — which part will the light hit? How far will the light go? What you have to keep in mind is where the light source is coming from. If the light is far above, the shadow will be shorter: if the light is lower the shadow will become longer. It's also worth remembering the shape of the object on which you are applying a shadow. Every shape has its own unique cast. The triangle has a pointy shadow, the circle has a circular shadow, the cylinder has a rectangular shadow, and the square has an 'L'-like shadow.

Inking

Inking is by far the most important skill that a manga artist needs to master. Although it is very similar to a pencil, a pen requires much more precision and patience. However, the rules that apply to pencilling also apply to inking, so let us look at the basic skills of drawing lines before anything else.

The most crucial skill of drawing is to learn to control the thickness and consistency of the line you draw. Drawing nice, clean lines sounds perfectly easy, but this is a skill that takes lots of time to master.

The ability to produce clean lines originates from two aspects – arm control and pressure.

A mistake that beginners often make while learning to draw is using only the wrist during the drawing process. In order to produce nice lines, you must use your entire arm. Using the entire arm increases control, thus producing straighter, more confident lines. Granted it is not easy, (your arm will hurt for a while), but nevertheless, it's a skill that has to be mastered.

A good practice in using your arm for drawing is to draw vertical or horizontal lines across a moderately sized sheet of paper. You will immediately notice that it is easier to draw clean, straight lines when you use your entire arm. Thickness is determined by two factors: angle and pressure. The angle of the pen or pencil to the surface of the paper is proportional to the area that the tip comes in contact with the paper. Therefore, altering the angle of your pen can easily alter the thickness. In the case of a ballpoint or nib pen, an angle closest to 90° will produce the thinnest line. This is usually true for a pencil also, but since the tip becomes dulled fairly fast in a pencil, the point may not be at the center.

Pencils should be rotated to keep the same thickness and avoid over-sharpening.

Pressure influences nib pens and pencils but has little or no effect on ball-points. Controlling the amount of strength exerted on the pen/pencil also takes a lot of practice. In general, a pen or pencil requires only a small amount of force to produce nice lines. Unnecessary pressure not only draws thick, unclean lines, but it will also ruin the tip. Try drawing quicker, lighter strokes to avoid exerting too much pressure.

A manga drawing is not truly complete until it has at least been inked. There are two major methods of inking that I am familiar with. The first is inking digitally with the computer. The other method is by hand with actual pens. This is the more traditional way of inking, and still the most popular.

The best way to ink by hand is with an inking kit. These usually consist of a special pen with a slit in the end for a pen nib. Nibs come in many different styles and sizes, all designed to be dipped in a bottle of ink.

The results from an inking kit can be second to none, but if you can't face getting to grips with nibs and a bottle of ink then never fear. There are some superb felt tips pens available that will produce excellent results. They come in a range of sizes, produce beautiful clean lines, won't splatter and you can get a decent set for under $20! However, watch out if you're left-handed as you may smudge the lines you draw.

No matter what type of pen you use, you will need to trace your sketch. You can either take the sketch itself and ink the sketch directly, then, using a soft eraser, rub the pencil lines away. Or you can get a 'light box' and trace the picture on to a new piece of paper. This second option might be preferable for the beginner as you don't run the risk of ruining your original sketch.

QUICK TIP!

Rushing your inking might leave mistakes, or unwanted and stray lines, so take your time.

SCAN & CGING

...NING

What is CGing? CG is short for Computer Graphics. Sometimes you'll hear CG being referred to as CGI, which means the same thing, Computer Generated Imagery. CG and CGI are broad ranging terms that cover any type of artwork that's made on a computer. From a scratchy image put together in Windows Paint, to a manipulated and edited photo in Adobe Photoshop, these are all examples of CG.

This section is not 'an everything you need to know about CGing' – we'd need a whole book for that! But I will cover some aspects, from scanning and cleanup to coloring, to provide a very basic foundation in CG artwork.

Why CG? Have you ever heard anyone say, 'Everything's going to computers'? That's partially the case here, and there's a good reason why. Computers are capable of so much! Over the years computers have evolved into tools for a vast range of different uses. At first, computer graphics were simplistic and fake looking. Graphics software had to be written in house and was hard to understand and utilize. Nowadays however, computers and their users are capable of producing imagery that looks just as good as traditional style artwork and better. Add that to the flexibility and functionality of computers and you've got a pretty good reason to make the jump to CG.

SCANNING & COLORING   SCANNING & CGing

Scanning

It's important to be able to transfer your pictures into a digital format on the computer without losing any of the original quality. It's also good to know how to enhance your images to make them look cleaner and sharper than your original artwork.

A scanning menu or window appears. Set the scanner to 300dpi (dots per inch) and 50% or 100% print size. I usually use 50%, as I only have 120MB of RAM on my PC. Unfortunately, PhotoShop has a tendency to crash if you have really large files and not enough RAM. There are two reasons for scanning at 300dpi instead of 100 or 70.

Firstly, the scanned image will show up clearer because the scanner is picking up more individual dots from the artwork, and the more detail picked up, the more accurate the image is. Another reason is that if you intend to color the work it's always best to start out with a large sized picture so you can color fine details close up and at a decent image resolution. You can then adjust the size of the image if you intend to publish it on the web etc.

If the scanned image is very small, it will be a lot harder to color and the final image quality will be poor.

Make sure that the scanner lid is firmly down. I usually leave a heavy weight on it while it scans, so there's always an even pressure being applied to the scanned piece of work. If you were to hold the lid down manually and you were shaking, the scanned lines might come out looking crooked. The closer the image is to the scanner's glass, the more detail the scanner will be able to pick up.

Sometimes if the scanner lid isn't shut properly, outside light can get in and reflect on the image, which further reduces scan quality.

If scanning black and white line art, set the scanner to either Gamma 1.0 or Gamma 1.5. You'll get slightly better results depending on the scanner and what type of work you are scanning. Make sure the scanner is scanning in GRAYSCALE and not B/W (black and white) or RGB /CYMK (color) The bad thing about B/W is that the scanned lines are black and white pixels only, and the lines are not anti-aliased. The downside of RGB is that the scanner will pick up unnecessary colors, when all you want is the black and white line art.

If your picture takes up more than the scanner's surface area, you will need to scan it in two halves and join it up later. Once again, while scanning, make sure the lid is pressed down where the second half overlaps or you'll end up with a big, faded gray area near the edge of the scan. Though this is important, don't press down REALLY hard so that it leaves a great big crease in the middle of the work. After scanning the first piece, scan the next with exactly the same settings as the first (300dpi, gray scale etc).

Summary

- Set scanner to 300dpi at 50 or 100% print size

- Make sure the scanner lid is firmly down

- Scan at a Gamma level to suit your artwork, usually Gamma 1.0 for ink work and 1.5 for pencil

- Scan in grayscale

Cleaning-Up

Now after I've scanned my work into Photoshop, I'll need to clean it up.

The first task is to adjust the levels: Image -Adjust - Levels (CTR+L). Just spend a bit of time tweaking the gamma levels until the lines look nice and dark and the white background goes pure white without any discoloration or smudges being visible.

You might prefer the look of really dark lines if you've just scanned in some pencil work, or you might like to keep it lighter like the original. It's personal preference really. I usually go for something twice as dark as my original sketches because I usually draw with a 2H pencil.

Alternatively you might want to fiddle around with the brightness and contrast: Image -Adjust - Brightness. I've seen so many pictures that could have looked twice as good if only the artist had spent time cleaning up the image and making the lines look sharper, so it's very important to prepare the image in the correct way whether you wish to color it or not.

Sometimes when you scan, the image won't appear dead straight, so you might want to adjust and rotate the canvas slightly. Usually I'd adjust the canvas size of my image making it slightly bigger around all the edges by 100 pixels or so. Then Image -Rotate canvas -Arbitrary, then rotate CW (clockwise) or ACW (Anti clockwise) from 0.4 degrees to 4 degrees, or however much you need to get the image lined up perfectly. Now you'll want to crop the image.Using the crop tool is ideal to get rid of any surplus border. It's always a very good idea to crop a picture down to size if there's a lot of unnecessary blank space.

SCANNING & CGing

SCANNING & COLORING

There might be a few smudges or random dark unwanted pixels still on the image. To get rid of these use the pencil or paint-brush tool and color white over those areas. To clear any mess out of small nooks and crannies, you might want to try using the Pixel selection tool, then simply fill in the selection you wish to clear with white, or just click Delete, but make sure white is also your secondary color if you do this.

Now your picture should be clean and looking good. If you don't want to color in the line work and wish to now save your image, adjust the image size: -Image -Image size. You'll possibly want no more than a pixel width of 500 pixels, but it depends on whether your image has lots of detail or not. I suppose you'll have to be the judge of what image size looks best for your particular picture, but have a look at other artwork sites on the web and see what sort of sizes they use for their pictures. You can do this by right clicking the full sized image and select-ing Properties.

To join up two separate images, adjust the canvas size (-Image -Canvas size) of scan #1 to little over double and make sure to have white selected as your secondary color. Now go back to scan #2, select the layer Background in the layers tab and drag this layer on top of scan #1. Use the drag tool to move scan #2 so it fits in perfectly (or nearly) next to scan #1. A good tip when adjusting the position of scan #2 is to zoom in at 100% and get the lines flush with scan #1. If the lines simply refuse to join up properly, you might need to rotate Scan #2: -Edit -Transform - Rotate. Use trial and error to very lightly rotate the layer and see if it joins up better after the rotation. After you've got it lined up flatten the image and go though the previous preparation process.

Summary

- Adjust the levels to achieve a sharper, cleaner look

- Rotate the canvas or image if the scan is not dead straight

- Crop the image

- Clean any extra smudges and pixels with the pencil and pixel selection tools

Coloring

If you want to digitally color your line work, there are many ways to do this. Here's a very simple method to get you started. To begin with, adjust the image mode to color: -Image -Mode -RGB. Then, in the layers tab, drag the background layer on to the 'new layer' icon, which will create a copy of the background on to a clean and adjustable new layer (otherwise you won't be able to move the outlines on to the top in the layers tab).

Delete the bottom 'back-ground' layer and rename the 'copy of background' layer to 'outline'. Next, check the preserve trans-parency box for this layer.

While the outline layer is selected, go to the layer drop-down menu and select 'multiply'.

After that create a new layer and call it BG or Background. Now, on the background you'll be able to color underneath the

If you draw anything that includes nature, get some nature books. Or look at the nature around you. Many people draw trees in the same way or use the same colors – brown and green. Have a look – you will notice there's more to trees than brown and green!

QUICK TIP!

These illustrations show the simple steps from initial drawing to completed color picture

lines of the outline layer, but on top of the white of the outline layer!

Alternatively go to the channels tab and click the circular channel selection icon. The image should be filled with dotted lines. Next click delete – this will get rid of all white areas. Deselect the channel selection and then move back to the layers tab. Since the preserve transparency box is checked you can then reapply black to the outlines by using the pencil tool with a brush size of 300+, then going over the whole picture to restore black to the outlines. Create a new layer underneath called BG or background and you'll be able to color underneath the remaining outlines!

Summary

- Change image mode to RGB

- Turn the background layer into an adjustable outline layer

- Multiply the layer, then color underneath

- OR:

- Delete the white area of the outline layer by using the channel selection icon

- Then re-color the black lines with the pencil tool while preserve transparency is checked.

Photoshop – tools/basics

The following tutorial covers the basics of learning PhotoShop in relation to 'CGing' or comic book and anime style coloring. There's more than just one style of coloring. Keep in mind what you want to achieve. If you're already familiar with PhotoShop, then this might not be as helpful, but you might still pick up a few tips.

For this tutorial I'm using PhotoShop 6 on a PC, but most tools are the same as earlier versions of the program.

Ok, so you want to CG color your line artwork or line art and have just discovered PhotoShop is the thing to do it. The package is used in all sorts of illustration and graphic design fields, and most importantly, industry standard comic books!

The tool bar is very similar to Microsoft's 'Paint', so I'm sure you're familiar with the layout and interface. First I'd recommend checking out the 'Tool Bar overview' in the PhotoShop help (F1). Some of the icons contained on the bar are very important, others not so important but most are used for a CG, so here's what they do:

Marquee tools (M)

I use these a lot for what I call 'post production'. When the CG is all finished, I'll add extra shapes (details) to backgrounds and foregrounds. Tip: To create an outline from your selection go to -Edit -Stroke (or right click, stroke) and choose the line width. The color of the line will be the same as the primary color selection. Also I'll use it to select individual frames (on a sequential page).

Move tool (V)

Moves selections, layers and painted areas. Useful, but I don't use it too often during a CG.

Lasso tools (L)

Like the marquee tool, but you have more control over the selections you make. This tool is used a lot for 'Cuts' and 'Cel style' solid tones. The Magnetic tool is rarely used. If you don't have a Graphics Tablet, you'll spend more time with the Polygon tool, since the Freehand tool can be tricky to use with a mouse. When I lay my initial flat base tone, this is one of the three possible tools I'll choose to use. After you've made your selection, fill it with color. I often make amendments to my selections, so if you've made a mistake hold down SHIFT to add extra selections to your first selection – it's very handy. Use ALT to take away from your selection. You'll notice the – and + signs as you hold down the keys.

SCANNING & CGing

PHOTOSHOP

Magic wand tool (W)

Don't be fooled by the name! It won't do your CG for you!! Mostly used if you have some really clean, inked lines to work with for laying flats. Select an area in your drawing with the tool, then -Select -Modify -Expand. Expanding the selection will avoid a filled flat from looking as though it's all scummy around the edges. At the resolution I work at, I'll usually expand an extra 4-6 pixels without my selection going over the lines. Very thin lines might not work with this method, plus you might need to SHIFT add with the other selection tools to reach areas that the wand cannot get to.

Crop tool (C)

Only used at the very end to trim your finished art, or if your scan needs clipping back.

Slice tool (K)

Never needed it!

Airbrush tool (J)

I use it A LOT. After I've laid down my flat tones, I use this to render those tones. The best bit of advice I can give for this tool is to set the tool options to a low pressure. Something between 5-10% avoids an excess flow of paint and possibly a muddy looking rendered tone. Taking your time and using subtle shades will create a better result.

Paintbrush tool (B)

It's used a lot for Cel style in conjunction with the polygon lasso tool. It's also another method for laying down flats. When I use this tool I set the hardness to 100 and spacing to 1 for solid, clean brush strokes.

Pencil tool (B)

(With same icon as paint brush). I've only really used a size 999 to quickly reapply a flat tone on a locked layer if I've made a mistake and want to start again.

Clone stamp tool (S)

Never needed it, but I could see it coming in handy for SFX.

History brush tool (Y)

This brush and I don't have much history between us – never used it.

Eraser tool (E)

I use this one a fair bit. A good tip is to use it on a locked layer tone so that the secondary color selection is used. It saves time swapping and picking a second color because I have my tablet pen button set to eraser.

Gradient tools (G)

DON'T try to rely on these instead of an airbrush. The only thing I'd use them for is part of a background. Generally these are what slackers use that think they're CGing.

Paint bucket tool (G)

(With same icon as gradient). Used for filling selections in with flat tones, nothing else.

Blur tool (R)

Occasionally used to help bend colors and to get rid of seams.

Sharpen tool (R)

(With same icon as blur) Hardly ever used.

Smudge tool (R)

(With same icon as blur.) Used a little more often than the blur tool and takes a lot of memory to use. Sometimes you'll need a really high spec PC to use a large smudge brush, and even then it'll take 5 minutes to apply the change!

Dodge tool (O)

I've seen people achieve excellent, more realistic looking results with this tool, but it's difficult to handle and achieve a more subtle graded tone. I'd recommend using it on 50% pressure or less and apply it to Midtones.

Burn tool (O)

(With same icon as dodge.) The opposite to Dodge, but used less. I'd rather start with a dark tone, then get lighter with dodge, than start with a middle tone and use both dodge and burn.

Sponge tool (O)

(With same icon as dodge.) Alters the amount of 'pigment' on a rendered tone. I've never really needed it.

Path selection tools (A)

Never used it, since I don't use paths very often.

Type tool (T)

Adds text! Usually just for post-production or details on a character.

Pen tools (P)

Similar to the polygon lasso (dot-to-dot style selection), but you have a lot more control over it. I never use it.

⬚ ⬭ ⬚ ◇ ╲ Custom shape tool (U)

Most important is the line tool, which draws straight lines. Not used much.

🗔 🔊 Annotations tool (N)

I can't see how this would be at all useful unless you're just really bored!

🖊 Eyedropper tool (I)

I usually use it every time I CG. It's easiest if you select a brush. If you're painting with that brush and notice you need to grab some color from your canvas, hold ALT and the brush changes to the eyedropper.

🖐 Hand tool (H)

I use the scroller on my mouse to move up and down an image or just use the scroll bars on the right and bottom of the window.

🔍 Zoom tool (Z)

I zoom in and out of my images a lot, but never do it via the tool icon. Just use CTRL and + or – instead, much easier!

So now you know what the tools do, you'll need to know what layers are.
Layers work like sheets of acetate – you know, like they use in animation? The stuff you paint on to one layer won't affect another layer in the layer tab. If you paint on a layer above the one below, you'll cover up the bottom layer BUT not paint over it. Go to the PhotoShop Help (F1) and read the info on layers, while experimenting on your own. Layers are a very important part of the CGing process and you need to know how you use them and how they work.

Once you've laid your flat tone, it's ready for CGing, so lock it. By locking that layer, it effectively creates a mask so you can only paint on the flat and nothing else, which is the best thing about layers! By putting different colors on different layers, you can render each individually without adding unwanted color on to the girl's face or tone on the guy's jacket. I could write a book on layers and CGing alone, but PhotoShop's Help files have the same info and practice really will make perfect!

Summary

I hope this gives you an idea of the tools involved in coloring your work with PhotoShop. There are similar programs such as PaintShop Pro, which is a great alternative if you can't get hold of PhotoShop.

STORYB

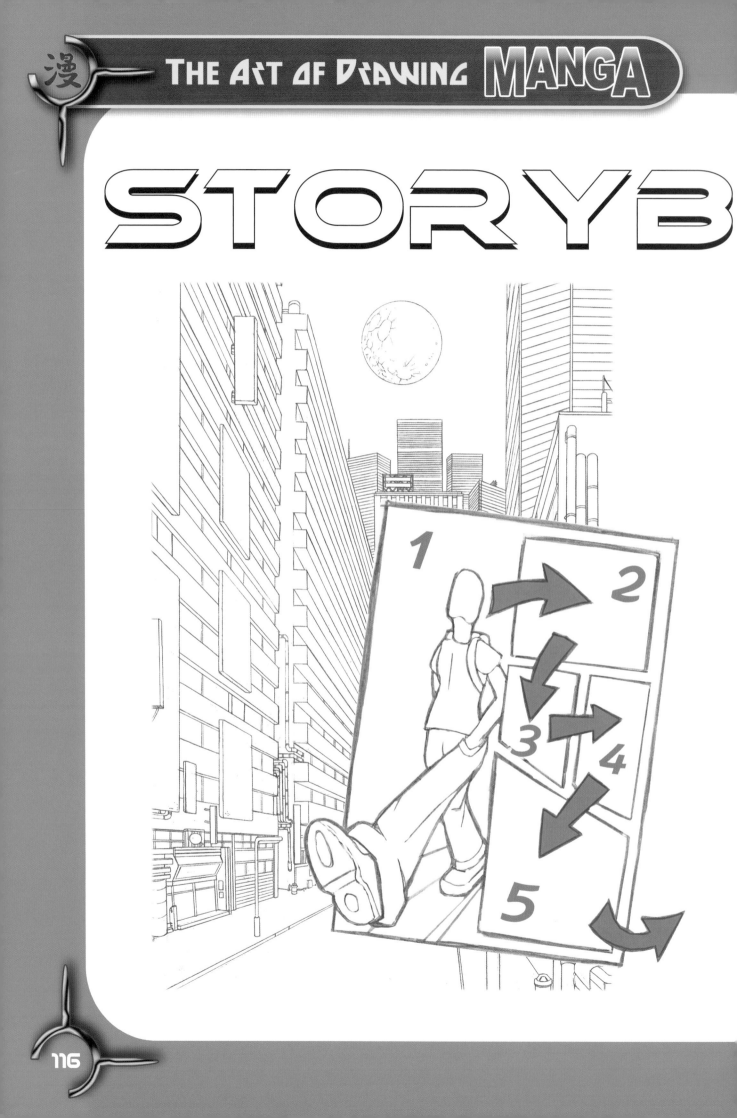

⊃ARDING

There is nothing better than taking a character you've created and putting them in their own comic strip. However, this can be a very time consuming process and also hard work! Here are a few useful things to remember:

The first and most important lesson when drawing a manga page is – don't waste too much time on setup. Every page that you waste on boring setup brings the whole project closer to being a dull end product. Ideally, the setup at the beginning of the comic is either so brief it fits on a few pages or, even better, in a few panels. You could also throw it out as a text-only prologue or even just flash back to it later. Either way, do the bare minimum of setup and get to the meat of the story as quickly as possible.

You need to keep several things in mind while figuring out the page layout. For example, you should remember that a manga describes action. Thus, timing is important. Another aspect to keep in mind is the importance of the panel that you will be drawing. How much impact does the panel carry? In general, the bigger panels attract more attention than smaller ones. Therefore, big panels should be reserved for important scenes that need emphasis while the small ones are used for panels that aid the fluency among the panels.

Over the next few pages you'll find an example of a storyboard – I hope it helps.

Ideally, the setup for your panels should always be brief and to the point, each page telling its own important part of the overall story.

Have a look at the panels opposite – this is a classic setup for a western comic page, with the reader reading across from left to right. Plan out your whole story before you begin so you know exactly what will appear in each panel – remember, the fun is in the drawing, not agonizing over whether you've got enough panels!

It's a mistake to draw a manga page without writing the script in advance and storyboarding it as well. But don't waste your time planning/writing scenes dozens of pages in the future. It just saps your energy from actually drawing the current pages, and by the time you get there your hard work will probably be obsolete anyway.

Start sketching your panels out very roughly to see how they hang together on the page.

STORYBOARDING

It's important to keep the story moving at all times – a dead panel makes for a dull story! Basically, if you're not interested in drawing some event, just have a character allude to it and keep going.

With the panels here I'm setting up a cliffhanger ending, forcing the reader to want to get to the end of the page. Who's the boy? Where is he? What's he doing? Why is that dangerous looking character following him? Is that a knife? As a comic book artist you are constantly building expectation and tension, drawing the reader into the plot.

Notice how the first panel gives you the big picture, but without any of the detail. It is the smaller, more precise panels that unfold events.

It's a good idea to draw as big as possible! It's easy to draw details on a huge sheet of paper, but adding tiny details on a small character can be very awkward.

QUICK TIP!

Writers often use the phrase 'murder your darlings' – this refers to beautifully written scenes, or characters, that writers are loathe to cut even though they don't add to the story as such. Cutting these elements is even more important in comics than in prose. Sure, it may sound great now, but when it comes to the time to draw it, and draw it, and draw it... you'll be tearing your hair out halfway through from boredom. And if it bores you, think of what it'll do to your readers.

Cut mercilessly to the 'good stuff' as soon as possible on the page. Similarly, if you find yourself writing basically the same dialogue twice — for example, a situation that has to be explained a couple of times to different characters — you're doing something wrong.

Look at how this is now coming together. As the artist (and storyboarder) you are implying a particular turn of events. Is your friendly, happy, harmless teenager about to be attacked for no reason by a knife-wielding maniac? What will happen? The reader has to turn the page to find out. It is very important to create this element of suspense with your images.

Alternatively the boy could have dropped his knife and the other guy is chasing after him to give it back. But this seems unlikely given the way the characters have been drawn. Your work on expressions and figures will come in extremely handy here!

Notice how this whole plot has been created without using one single word of text, and yet the reader knows exactly what is going on. We can now use coloring to hit home a few points. The 'good guy' is wearing bright colors to match his cheerful disposition. He has no worries and no enemies.

The 'bad guy', on the other hand, is wearing black, has dark hair and shadows around his eyes. Look at those sharply raised eyebrows – scary! Notice as well how the technique of foreshortening is used to make the knife seem much larger and more frightening than it actually is.

I've also used action lines to suggest the speed and surprise of the 'attack', and a lens flare on the knife to give it a wicked glint.

If you feel you have no new ideas for drawings, redraw your old sketches – you'll be pleasantly surprised by the improvement, and hopefully it will give you the inspiration to get over your creative block!

QUICK TIP!

Here is where you bring it all together. The gray, industrial coloring of the background ties in with the gritty, dangerous situation of the storyline. The teenage boy seems out of place roaming these shadowy, deserted streets. But the man in black seems perfectly at home in this dark environment. It becomes clear who is the outsider.

In just five panels we have created an exciting, suspenseful plot, with interesting characters and a great cliff-hanger. Everything in these pictures helps build the story, from the expressions to the coloring.

Try your own storyboard – it's a fantastic way to get the most from your character creations.

STORYBOARDING

CREAT
CHARA

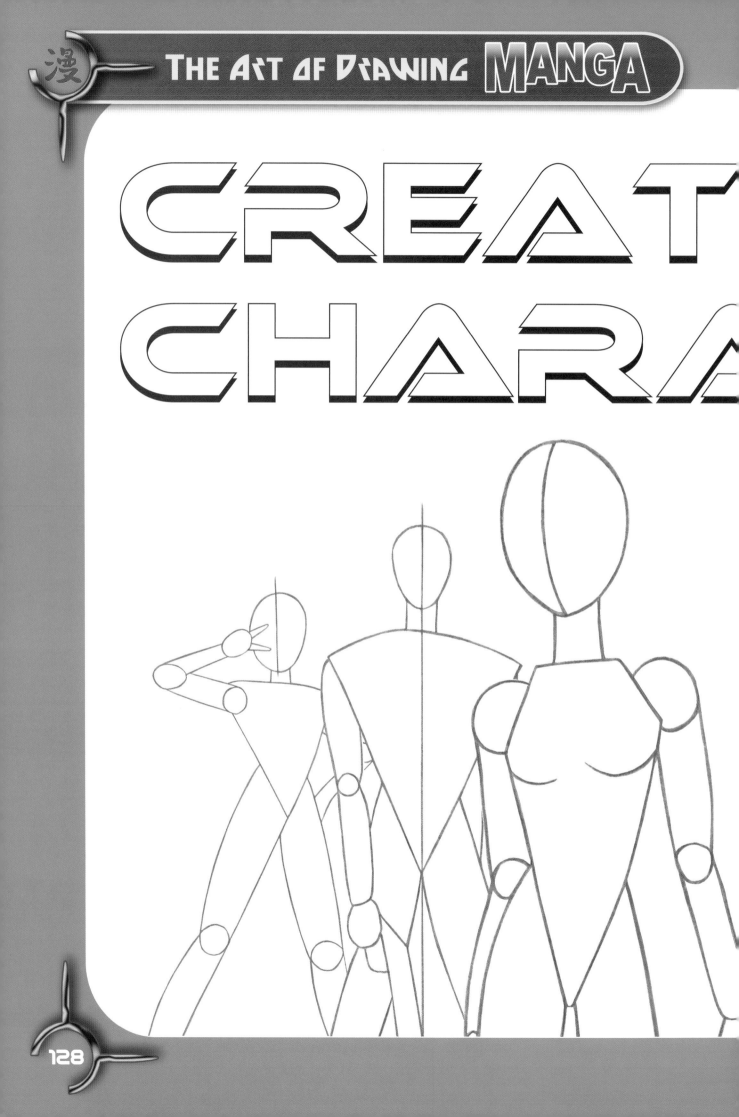

Manga style is instantly recognizable and since the release of Katsuhiro Otomo's cult classic AKIRA in the west in 1988, many comic artists have been inspired to pick up a pencil and give it a try themselves. Hopefully you are now one of them too!

In this book you have seen how to construct characters and how to put them into settings and comic book panels. The character is undoubtedly the main focus of any manga or anime so practicing how to create and draw these effectively is the first step for any aspiring manga artist. Consequently, it has been the main focus of this book and hopefully you have found the numerous tips, guides and examples helpful.

Throughout the book the emphasis has been on drawing from real life and referring to existing objects and people for your designs. Although stylized, all anime creations are taken from current/past objects and the designs around us. For example, a twenty-fourth century spaceship may be based on a nineteenth century paddle steamer and a hero's spiky hair may have been inspired by a garden shrub. Look out for things like this in existing manga and keep an eye out for similar objects you could reference to inspire your own creations.

Now it's time to gather up your materials, find a clear workspace and start producing your own creations. I hope the characters on the following pages provide plenty of inspiration!

CHARACTER CREATION

A big part of developing a character is knowing what kind of body language they use. A big mistake beginners make when drawing pin-ups of their characters is to ignore the personality of the character they are doodling. I often see illustrations posted by artists that have a character standing with a weapon like they are sitting in a Sears studio for family photos...NO! Try and avoid using the normal stance. Think about your character...think about what it is your character does and what effect that would have on the way they carried themselves. Are they graceful? Are they clumsy? Do they laugh, skip, play or mope, drag and cry? Picture this in your head before you put the pencil to paper. You can say a lot with just a stick figure. Get your stick figure exactly right before you flesh in your character. A good foundation is important if you want your piece to have the right impact.

Check these examples of some creations to help you along your way.

CUTS OFF DRAGON HEAD/NECK

BENGONIN BENGOSHA "DEFENDER"

BOMU! 2002

ボム

FORE→ ARM BLADE (DETACHABLE)

SHOULDER SPIKES SHOOT OUT

MURUSAME!

Here I've put together a complete drawing of my new creation and started playing around with ideas before finalizing the character. It's always worth taking time to play with ideas before completing your drawing.

MURASAME KATANA
ムラサメ カタナ
BENGO SHA
ベンゴシヤ
BE N GO SHA
べんご

Sometimes it can be a good idea to plan out more complicated scenes or poses before you draw them properly. I sometimes draw 4 or 5 thumbnail sketches to plan out just one picture. It can save a lot of time in the long run by getting rid of your mistakes at an earlier stage.

QUICK T

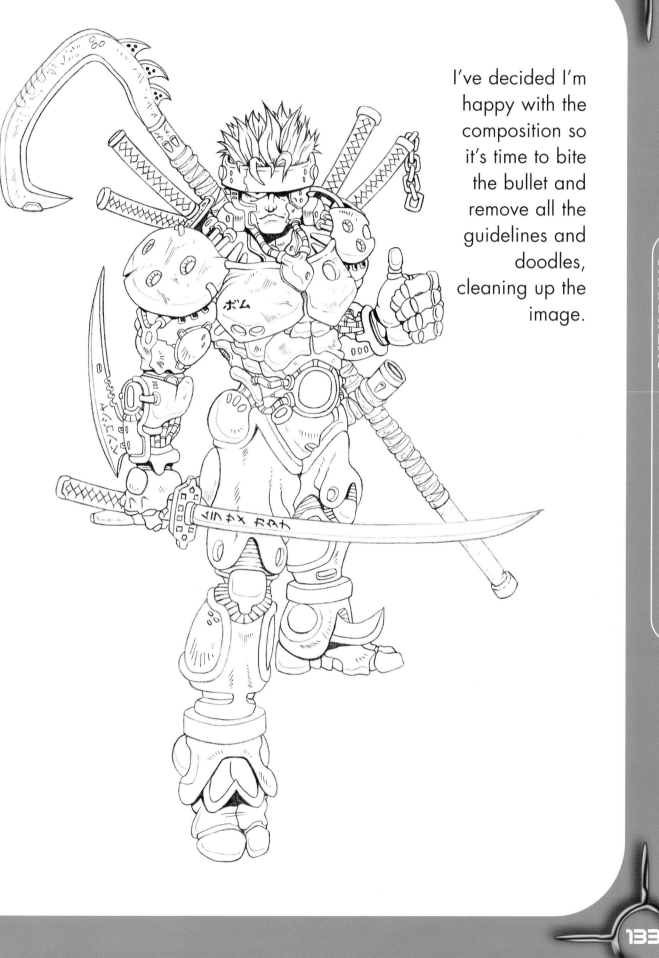

I've decided I'm happy with the composition so it's time to bite the bullet and remove all the guidelines and doodles, cleaning up the image.

Inked in and fully colored this is him in all his glory! Pretty cool.
There are a number of influences on the look of this character, and he's very much a combination of samurai warrior and mecha...

BENGOSHA

He's Bengosha – Japanese cyborg warrior from the future where monsters, demons and dragons have become a real problem in Tokyo after a parallel dimension portal opened up in Shinjuku 100 years ago! His father was a world famous Samurai master of Yosake Dojo and the secret owner of the legendary Murasame sword. After his father died in battle while he was still a boy, Bengosha inherited the Murasame and now acts as an elite defender of Tokyo.

Name: Bengosha
Weight: 265lbs
Height: 6 feet 5 inches
Weapons: Murasame Sword

If you look very carefully you'll notice that these lovely ladies are all very similar in terms of facial features and physique.

It therefore makes you realize how important the details – such as hair, clothes and accessories – can be in developing personalities and individual characteristics in your creations.

TEMPEST TRIPLETS

These battling teens are not just pretty faces. When their younger brother was badly injured in an unprovoked attack by a rival high school, the triplets took it upon themselves to seek justice, vowing to find those responsible. The trail led to the notorious Ring of Skulls Gang and a showdown with their ringleader Cranium. Using a combination of ju-jitsu and street fighting, the triplets defeated Cranium and avenged their brother. They now continue their role as righters of wrongs, meting out justice as the Tempest Triplets for those who have no other recourse .

Name: Miki, Aoki, Haruka

Age: 16

Height: 5 feet 5 inches

Weight: 116lbs each

School: Yukada High

Fighting Skill: Ju-jitsu and street fighting

There's not a lot I can say about Nikki, although the use of color was very important in getting the illustration just right! This was a Christmas card I designed and it brought a lot of cheer to those who received it! Joking aside, you can see many of the techniques I mentioned earlier, such as the shaping of the hair, the use of speculars, the folds of the clothes and the importance of facial expressions.

NIKKI

Nikki is the ultimate stealth operative! A famous fashion model she is in demand around the world, but her high profile lifestyle also gets her close to the rich, famous and influential, and proves the perfect cover for her real skills as a seeker and seller of information. People underestimate Nikki at their peril!

Name: Nikki
Age: 24
Height: 5 feet 6 inches
Weight: 120lbs
Occupation: Spy for hire
Skills: lock-picking, hacking, smuggling
Equipment: just her charm!

CREATING CHARATERS

RUDY ROUGHNIGHT

What can you tell about Rudy's background or personality from this picture? Little features can make all the difference. What does the band-aid signify? Is Rudy a fighter or did he cut himself shaving? Is the frown one of aggression or confusion?

RUDY ROUGHNIGHT

Rudy is actually a character from the RPG Wild Arms.

Rudy is a young Dream Chaser who was exiled from the town of Surf because of his mysterious weapon, the ARM. When he was a young boy, Rudy was much stronger than any regular child, so he was feared and became alone, finding comfort only in the house of his grandfather, Zepet. He is one of the few people in the world who can synchronize with the ARMs, making him a forceful fighter.

Name: Rudy Roughnight

Age: 15

Height: 5 feet 8 inches

Weight: 160lbs

Companions: Jack and Cecilia

Weapon: sword

Greatest fear: remaining in exile